T0115204

WHEN HE Whispers

Learning to Listen on the Journey

LINNEA BOESE

WESTBOW
PRESS®
A DIVISION OF THOMAS NELSON
& ZONDERVAN

WestBow Press books may be ordered through booksellers or by contacting:

WestBow Press
A Division of Thomas Nelson & Zondervan
1663 Liberty Drive
Bloomington, IN 47403
www.westbowpress.com
844-714-3454

Interior Image Credit: Tom Harpootlian; Linnea Boese

Scripture quotations taken from The Holy Bible, New International Version® NIV® Copyright © 1973 1978 1984 2011 by Biblica, Inc. TM. Used by permission. All rights reserved worldwide.

ISBN: 978-1-6642-2410-0 (sc)
ISBN: 978-1-6642-2409-4 (e)

Print information available on the last page.

WestBow Press rev. date: 04/15/2021

Dedicated to my partner in life and ministry,
Glenn Boese,
who has helped me with technical issues
and constant encouragement.
His patience with this bookworm and pen-in-hand listener
is one of the reasons I have been free to devote my time
to listening, and to putting this all together.

Many thanks to Amber Beery,
for the gift of her time to edit the manuscript,
and to Tom Harpootlian,
for his beautiful photos to illustrate the poems.
(Three photos were taken in Africa by me, pp. 30, 80 and 98)

Contents

Introduction xi

1. LEARNING TO LISTEN xv
Waiting for Word 1
Be Silent 3
Finding Him in the Noise 5
Grateful, Listening 6
Solitude at the Beach 7
If He Comes 8
Time Apart 11
His Face 14
Other Food 16
The Throne of Grace 17
In the Silence... 19
One Sure Thing 21
Shouts of Joy..23

2. WAITING – OR NOT 27
Cones and Reservoirs...29
Ant Lions 30
Cave 32
The Shape of You...34
Contemplation 36
The Alert Wait 37
Waiting for Dawn in the Grove 38
Waiting for the Master...40

3. WHAT HE SAID 41

Fixed Thoughts 43

Hang in There, He Said 45

All I Have is Yours 46

Praying Hosea 11 47

Open Up or Hold Back? 48

Prayer Wrestler 50

New Clothes 52

4. WHEN IT'S HARD 55

Download 57

Psalm on Mean Street 59

Refuge 62

Pressure 64

I Am That Ewe 66

Turning the Other Cheek 68

In the Wind 69

The Cleansing 71

The Watched Pot 73

The Rain 74

5. HEARING THE VOICE IN NATURE 77

Look Up 79

Higher Things 81

Reminder to My Soul 83

What I Would Rather Be 84

This Is What I Hear Today 85

Morning Shade 86

Morning Hope 87

Daybreak Shower 89

Cool Breeze 91

Stillness 92

6. THE CONVERSATION..95
When I Pray 97
Prayer Circle: Jesus Intercedes 99
A Table Set Before Me...100
Mourning 103
Sensing God 104
Taste the Glory!..106

GLOSSARY (Note: individual words marked by italics are
included in the glossary.)..109

Introduction

As I launch this venture of sharing a very intimate pilgrimage with you readers, I want to challenge you to walk the journey with me. Some of you are way ahead of me in learning to listen to what the Lord says to you moment by moment. Some of you may be those right by my side. If you are someone who is finding this a time to concentrate on progress in listening, I hope you will be encouraged. I am still learning but am finding it more and more an essential element of being a true servant of my Lord Jesus Christ.

For over 40 years, my main occupation was in ministry in Ferkessédougou in northern Côte d'Ivoire, where my husband and I were serving with WorldVenture. The Lord had laid the least-reached Nyarafolo people on our hearts, and the story of the way that he led us into strategic relationships so that churches were planted, over the years, is yet another one to tell.

Along the way, one of the key things that I realized was the need for God's Word to be translated into the previously unwritten Nyarafolo language so that the people could understand what it actually says. So I got training in linguistics and biblical studies, worked with a team that the Lord put together one by one over time, and we did as much of that as was possible. This year, 2021, the Nyarafolo are receiving the print copy of the New Testament, Pentateuch and Psalms!

That translation project was truly an intense learning curve. I would spend my days learning the language (still in progress!), developing the writing system, figuring out the grammar, researching the terms for which it was a challenge to find clear translation solutions, discussing it all with my translation team. I would come home from the office across our courtyard in the evening and work hard at turning off the churning thought processes still pouring through my brain. In the morning I would often wake up with a solution! Or more questions to pose. The words that I so loved were becoming all-consuming.

Living far from where I might find physical mentors, my love of words took me into researching what I could do to maintain spiritual growth in the middle of what I began to call the "mud puddle" of words. I was intrigued by certain spiritual disciplines that kept rising to the surface: the practices of solitude, silence and listening. I began to call the first one "the solitude of two" because it involves finding a place away from distractions where one can be alone with the Lord. Adele Ahlberg Calhoun says in the *Spiritual Disciplines Handbook* (2005): "Solitude is a 'container discipline' for the practice of other disciplines" (p. 111). Her book is a treasure chest of descriptions of spiritual formation practices, one that truly assisted me in my journey. Another was Ruth Haley Barton's *Invitation to Solitude and Silence* (2010). In learning to be quiet in the Presence of the Lord, I began to learn to let the mud in the dense puddle of my thoughts settle. The words would keep swirling for a while, as though blown around by gusts of wind (I think the Breath of God), then gradually I would find silence possible. I could begin to wait, to listen for what the Lord might want me to hear that day.

My place of retreat was in the west side of my courtyard, separated from the busy town square and roads by a wall. Golden rain trees grew in the hard clay soil there, beside a range of mango trees. Birds came to perch in them each morning, to look for food or just call out their melodies.

I told my family and friends that Saturday mornings from 6 to 9 a.m. were my hours of retreat in what became my "sacred grove," and that I was not to be interrupted except if it were urgent. To my surprise, it worked! When traveling I had to be creative. What I found most helpful was to be beside the ocean or a river in the morning, or on a second-floor veranda in a city. Here in Detroit where we live in retirement, I have my morning space in the rehabbed attic, with candles inside and a lovely view of trees and rooftops outside.

But the key goal has been to hear God's voice. It was also a conversation. I learned to praise him, to be thankful. I poured out my distresses. He is an excellent listener, and just doing that opened my heart to be ready to hear what he would answer. There were moments of joy and of lament, moments of confession and repentance, times when the Bible itself would come to mind with new meaning and others when nature was where I saw truth or hope. And I found that when I picked up my pen and little notebook, the words that flowed were often not what I expected. It was as if I were taking notes on a lecture or, more accurately, on the whisper in the ears of my heart. I am not saying that I heard an audible voice. But as I wrote, I felt that I was more sensitive to what the Spirit was impressing on me.

Being who I am, it was usually in the form of prose poetry that the words went on paper. I realize that we are each unique, and most of you probably "listen" in some other way than that. I've found it exciting to hear from friends how they have learned to recognize the nudges from the Lord as they read, walk, run, or listen to music.

Here I am exposing gleanings from the twenty-plus years of my own learning cycle in this domain. My prayer is that it will encourage many as they walk their path to increasing intimacy with Abba, through the Breath of the Counselor and the companionship of Jesus our Lord.

∼ 1 ∼

LEARNING TO LISTEN

∿ Waiting for Word
(1 Ki 19:8-15)

The prophet stood at the mouth of the cave,
waiting for God. Waiting for him to say something.
Forty days of running on the strength of heavenly food
had been stunning. But where was God?
Then the Word came, asking him a strange question:
What was he doing? Didn't God know, the one who
chose him, sent him, left him lonely in the crowd
of God-haters, prophet-killers?

The only word was to move again, to the summit.
There, on top of the mountain, the one man stood,
and the Presence was strong, but silent.
A gale whipped him from behind, tearing into the rocks,
ripping them into boulders. But that was not the LORD.
Why not? The winds of judgment are all his;
he makes the winds his messengers.
And there would come a day when
the sound of a violent wind would bring the Spirit.
But not this time.

He waited, and the ground beneath his feet shivered
as pieces of rock slid across the mountain slope
and rolled away. Cracks appeared; trees shuddered.
Earthquakes could announce openings between
earth and heaven, descent of angels,
rips in the fabric of the universe (as when,
one day, the Holy of Holies would be laid bare
and the door to heaven opened
as the King of kings was killed).

God might make clear his will in earthquakes.
But not this time.

Then there came a fire flaming high, passing by,
heating the air and shattered rock, lighting up the sky.
The prophet listened, waiting for the Voice, because
fire in a bush had called Moses, and Word had come.
A fiery pillar had led his people all night;
consuming fire had wiped away the rebels;
his glorious fire had covered the whole mountain
while he spoke his covenant Word.
But not this time.

The fire crackled, gently died away, and in the silence
of the mountain vastness, post-quake and post-wind,
there came a hush that shaped itself in Words.
The whisper overwhelmed him; the prophet lifted high
his cloak folds, desperate to cover his head, his face,
then stood at the cave entrance to meet his Lord.
There, in the sentient quiet of airy Breath,
the Word engaged him.

I seek you, too, the Present One, who always is,
and is with me. And sometimes it is wind and fire
and pillar-cloud and even quaking earth
that I desire, visible essence of your Presence.
But you choose your time, your place, your way,
to show me who you are, to speak into my soul.
And so I wait, and watch and listen, thanking you
for the glimpses, traces of your hand, and most of all,
the still small voice.

∼ Be Silent
(Ps 46:10)

The words come crashing in
like chattering kids.
They're only in my head
but they are deafening.

I cannot stem the tide.
A billion babblings
jostle for position.
One sinks, one bubbles up.

He urges silence,
and I long for quiet
to listen for his voice,
to know that he is God.

I'm desperate to hear him
through the clatter,
underneath the noise,
within the static.
Somewhere at a center point
is silence, deep inside
my cluttered cave.
And he is there.

∽ Finding Him in the Noise

You said you'd always be here,
even in the noise.
I dove within, and found you there
where you have always been.

There was a time when all I heard
were children's voices wanting mom,
and still you called me to connect
with you, beside my kids, at home.

Sometimes the stress is overwork,
or peopled hours and talk,
sometimes it's conflict that constricts
my heart and crimps my walk.

No matter where I am, or who
I'm with, what blasts my ear,
you're there and you are calling me,
if I just stop to hear.

∼ Grateful, Listening

Under the wet grass
crickets crick-crick.
Perched high near the sky
winged things sing melody.
If I don't pay attention
I miss the concert.

A rooster crows,
reminding me to listen.
A *coucal* adds her commentary,
counterpoint in alto.
Are you speaking, too,
and I'm just unaware?

The world is drenched
with your kind blessing.
I soak it in, on alert,
grateful, listening.

⌒ Solitude at the Beach

waves are crashing
      pushing to shore
white foam curves come
      licking up sand
birds in chorus are
      cheering the dawn
as light starts glowing
      to softly expand
and etch the horizon
      a straight gray line
and there come
      the fishing boats
all slipping west
      their flags whipped flat
while I sit watching
      exulting in rest
and listening
      softly yearning
for the Voice —
      this is the Best!

∼ If He Comes

if he comes with thunder
    a flash of light brighter than noon
        my eyesight will be shattered
            dis-illusioned by the brilliance
                and within I will be struck
                heart-wise
                    and be healed

if he comes in darkness
    a potent Presence out of sight
        I'll learn new ways of knowing
            grow sensors that can find him
                learn trust just like a baby
                and find out
                  he's light
                    in the dark

if he comes in showers
    drenching thirsty throats with life
        my soul will soak in love
            and grow in lushness
                flowering in time
                to grace this place
                with beauty

if he comes in whispers
    within what seems ordinary
        I'll follow every nudging
            by the practice of his Presence
              find new joy in obeying
              then receive
                  un-ordinary peace

if he comes with suffering
    holding me while pain chews me in two
    I'll find out what he meant
        by saying I would fill in turn
          his cup of sorrow
          to the brim
                become like him

if he comes in mystery
    with hints of holy secrets I can't bear
    I will learn to listen
        study tomes of wisdom
          ask him for discernment
        and discover
              growing is forever

if he comes in pleasure
        calling out my name with all the passion
        of an ardent lover
            I will open to him
                run into his arms
                    and stay
                        all his always

∿ Time Apart

1: Exodus 21:12-34

forty days forty nights
listening processing
all the world left behind
hearing Yahweh's voice

how to live how to give
following purposing
devotion the one thing
needed for his people

ripped apart from the start
spoken law broken law
Israel went their own way
trashed the One who saved them

2: Deuteronomy 9:18-10:11

forty days forty nights
face down hands down
all the world left behind
unglued for solitude

focused goal focused soul
listening petitioning
just one thing on his mind
mercy for his people

heart stirred God heard
reached out poured out
kindness and forgiveness
granting a new start

3: here and now

now I come here I stay
my goal his goal
seeking out time apart
to listen and to learn

how to rest how to grow
his way my way
begging for his mercy
on loved ones everywhere

a few hours a few themes
he's here I'm here
dealing with whatever
is before us in this day

∼ His Face
(Ps 27:8)

When I heard him say, "Seek my face,"
my heart skipped a beat like a goat leaping high
to land on a ledge then jump to the top
of a high crag, flat and shaded by pines,
to find him there, his face lit up
by the rising sun.

I wanted to ask him to share with me
some reasons behind all the suffering,
to draw me a map of the road laid out
for the coming days. But standing before him
I suddenly knew that one thing alone
was priority.
       So I bowed my heart
       and listened.

The fire of his Presence warmed my soul;
the light from his eyes swept clean
every cranny, the hoarded toys,
and I flew like a moth right into that flame
and found it health and life and love,
all dross removed.

To find his face is to be with him,
to know his heart and to rest, assured
that he rules the world and is wholly good,
that his Family is his true delight,
that he knows all about me
yet hugs me close.
Your face, Lord,
I will seek.

∾ Other Food
(Ps 63:5)

fasting
I find I'm not
at the mercy of my appetite

instead
you satisfy me
more than the richest of foods

manna
bread of heaven
bread of life broken for me

nourish
my flesh-bound soul
with words from the mouth of God

his mouth
to my heart
better than hot fresh cinnamon rolls

∼ The Throne of Grace
(Ps 131:2; Heb 4:16)

Frazzled, fragile,
wondering how I dare,
I climb the stairs
to the Majesty
(high on his throne,
watching the world)
and crawl onto his knees
(astonishing audacity).

He lays aside his scepter,
reaches for my arms,
pulls me to his lap,
whispers kindness
to my heart:
Dear daughter, rest!
Lay your head here,
on my chest.

He quiets me with love
while angels pause hosannas,
transpose into a melody
of simple adoration,
love songs. I feel
tension leak away.
My heart soaks in peace
as I pray.

Abba is aware of
every challenge,
every muddle,
each leap ahead.

He knows my life
from inside out:
claps hands with me,
sings, exults,
grabs me when I fall
and wipes my knees
when gravel bites,
loves me "even when."

Abba, Daddy, is the King,
his seat of power
the place where I
get all I need, and
nothing I deserve –
just precious words
of empathy, wise counsel
to show me how to be.

He gives kind gifts,
delicious treats,
new tools
so I can grow
and learn and laugh
and be his agent
in the field.

But just now
I keep my ear
close to his chest,
and rest.

⁓ In the Silence
(Zeph 3:17)

In the silence music pulses
calling me to leap to heaven,
join the Dancers in their passion—
Father, Son and Holy Spirit—
whirling universally,
twirling spheres and stepping high,
unison of glad abandon
freeing tempos in emotion
springing from the swirling ocean
climbing to the widest sky,
running with the flying sun
till the fire gilds the clouds,
holding hands and melding hearts,
one in integrated love.

Then the jubilation quiets
and the laughter shades to smiling
when he pulls me to his lap
in the potent celebration
of this flame that lights the stars
but remembers me with love,
holds me close to hear his song
of peace inside the silence.

∽ One Sure Thing

In this slippery tilting world
your heart is one sure thing.
You love me always, whether
I am striding straight ahead
or fallen in a thornbush,
listening raptly to your voice
or indulging my addictions,
desperately trying to feel good.

Unfailing love: *hesed*, the Hebrews said.
This is what we long for all our lives,
and this is Who you are.

We cannot shatter, dis-illusion,
wear away your tenderness.
You are love with no beginning
and no ending, always potent,
always steady, always ready to receive
the bullheaded son or daughter
who returns and finds in you
where the source of meaning is.

Your heartbeat never falters,
never skips a beat, or race
or turn erratic. You are life,
and I can crawl into your lap
or batter you with angry fists
or crucify you, tearing at your heart.
I've done it all, and more,
unfaithful to the core.

Yet you keep right on loving,
though I know you're disappointed
with this inner instability
and all the hurt it means for me.
I know you would be sad that
I would turn away from all that's good
and choose instead what turns to rot
and spreads infection through my soul.

The perfect Parent, you forgive.
And now I'm ready to accept
your happy smile when I succeed,
your loving hand-up when I fail,
your totally consistent love.
I cannot make you love me more.

Your love just IS. So I will dive into
the wonder of it all and live inside
unfailing love.

⁓ Shouts of Joy
(Ps 65)

I love you, Lord, my joy,
not for all you give
but who you are!
And yet your gifts
drench me in kindness.
Each one speaks
the soundless words
of a true lover
delighting in the search
for ways to slip
his message to me.
Joy wraps my moments,
weaves into my days:

> **Lights:**
> candle flickers, lamp glow,
> liquid moonlight, firefly stars,
> sunbeams shafting into gold,
> fires in my husband's eyes
> **Music:**
> my child's new song,
> mesmerizing *balophones*,
> rippling jazz, endless possibilities
> of tones and rhythms, harmonies
> **Laughter:**
> slapdash wordplays,
> comic kittens, shared delight,
> incredible good news
> spilling over into shouts

Shouts of joy, indeed,
the psalmist said, would be
our true response to wonder.
We mostly miss our cues,
I know. The days grind on,
our senses thickly cushioned
against pain but also joy,
for fear that it will prove
capricious, all too transient,
a brightly cloaked decoy.
The world stays dressed in gray
this safer way.

But I am sight-starved
for Reality.
Wash the windows clean, Lord!
Laser the lenses of my soul
until I see with clarity
all the love notes
left for me in hidden places
and right under my nose!

May I hope in you,
not in the sense
of "maybe" but "I know"
and freely gather joy
until, piles heaping,
these extravagant
provisions overflow
and bathe the hurts around me
with your healing balm.

And so, Lord, may
the inevitable gray
be streaked with light
in radiant jewel colors,
be swirled with melodies
and pulsing rhythms,
and always punctuated
by clear laughter
turning gladly into
shouts of joy!

~ 2 ~

WAITING – OR NOT

⁓ Cones and Reservoirs
(Ps 23:6, 131:2)

I sit by twenty tiny cones,

inverted, smoothed into the sand

so that some curious ant might step

into the trap, and slide downhill

to where the host lies hidden,

hungry.

       I'm waiting, too, for word from you

       but there's no need for craftiness.

       You wait until I'm ready, calm,

       having let go of stress and plans,

       happy to be against your chest,

       listening.

              And then I find the tables turned:

              You hunt me down, to hold me close,

              to wrap your love around my life,

              to plant your joy in reservoirs

              inside my soul, for when it comes—

              the testing.

∼ Ant Lions

the traps are there

silent

smooth slippery sand

lurking in my stomping grounds

waiting

for that moment when

(tired, stressed, stumbling)

I forget to watch

and slide

down that slope

into disaster

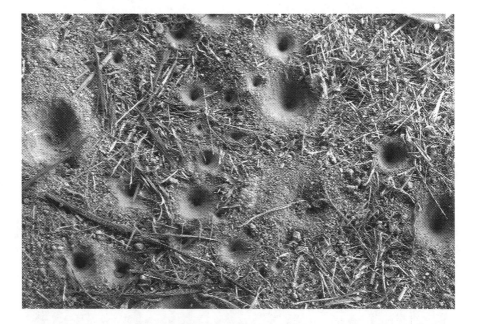

I let life take over
busy
pushing hard to meet my goals
eyes distracted by the rocks
obstacles I could climb over
holding Your strong hand
but
I lose my focus
stop listening to the Voice
step over the line
slip slam
my enemy just laughs

∼ Cave
(1 Ki 19)

after the marathon
(hard run finished)
fatigue was expected
but I caved in
spirit imploding
to a whimpering cry

the longed-for holiday
disappeared in
disappointment
and instead we
hit the road again
dodging potholes, driving on

(but all the way
my soul was washed
with music, its waves
lifting me to worship
by their movement
lapping at my sighs)
and now at home
my angel brings
me hearth cakes
(toast and coffee)
and gradually,
Elijah-like, I find my cave

so what is left
is listening for
whispers in the Word
and breathing in
soul-sustenance
of Spirit till restored

∼ The Shape of You

It's not that you weren't there before. But,
eyes not yet accustomed to blue dusk,
I could not focus. And so I thought you
absent, elsewhere, or unaware of me
and my excruciating need to hear you
audibly, the Voice that cries from heaven
or in whispers, and see you visibly,
a Person and a Presence I can locate
and can touch.

You're teaching me, so patient with
my slowness of perception, obtuseness to
your lessons. And it has dawned upon me
that the shape of you is one that I have known,
your silhouette the form that partnered me
in shadow, your warmth the arms that circled me
against the cold.

So when my eyes were opened, nerves made ready
by the longing and fine-tuned by healing mercy,
I began to sense your outline and the fragrance
of your nearness. I learned silence, hope of waiting,
yielding to whatever might be. And your love's flame
lit the stillness, reaching out to draw me to you.
Then I knew you, recognized the touch I've come
to treasure and the passion in your eyes:
the shape of you.

∿ Contemplation

I have read —
your words rang true,
and I saw your hand at work:
your love in history,
your ancient mystery.
    I lean back
    onto your chest
    to let you do what you will do:
    talk to me, sing to me,
    simply rock and hold me.

Abba God,
my ears feel plugged,
my inner eyes are restless!
I long to understand.
to feel your loving hand!
    I now wait,
    quieting the words,
    settling my questing heart
    in full submission:
    contemplation.

∼ The Alert Wait

The birds and I flit about
in this gray dawn
inspecting windfall treasures,
breathing the dense perfume
of damp earth
and occasional blossoms.

The trees wait in silence
for whatever happens next
and now so do I.
This day is one that God has made;
he has a plan,
and I will stay alert to it.

If winds blow and whip me,
may treasures fall about
for those in need.
Meanwhile I'll drink deeply
of the love soaking in
and pray that my aroma is a blessing.

⤳ Waiting for Dawn in the Grove

waiting for dawn
for crickets to sleep
and *bulbuls* to wake
to herald brand-new
sky-streaks with praise

waiting for light
to rise to the call
of roosters and dogs
shafts penetrating
shadows with hope

waiting for you
for your voice inside
to speak and unwrap
daunting enigmas
while I sing thanks

and when you come
you come in silence
under the hubbub
of motor rumblings
and metal clangs

with light so bright
it diamonds the dew
you turn leaves to neon
outline silken webs
with silver hue

bright white winged things
whirl in their dance
while I breathe Presence
and my yearning heart
wakes up to joy

∿ Waiting for the Master

The furball crouches patiently
on the carpet runner
just outside the bedroom door.
In a moment, maybe four,
his master will emerge.
The sun is coloring the air
with soft new light;
the dark is lifting. It is morning.

He will come.
He'll lift his little one,
caress the neck and ears.
There will be love.
There will be food.

Me, too. I wait,
catlike in the dawn,
watching for the light
and listening, knowing
he will come.

∼ 3 ∼

WHAT HE SAID

∼ Fixed Thoughts
(Phil 4:8)

Think, he said, about the truth:
what's known for sure
and stands its ground,
based on solid rock.
Not "maybe."

Think, he said, what's honorable:
What can you respect,
and meeting, recognize
as the best thing to do?
Not shady.

Think, he said, on all that's pure:
unadulterated,
clear all the way through
and undiluted.
Not dirty.

Think, he said, about what's lovely:
beauty where it lives
in line or word or action
or beloved one.
Not ugly.

Think, he said, what's admirable:
beyond the call of duty,
risk taken for the good
of someone else.
Not shoddy.

Think, he said, on excellence:
whole-hearted exercise
at work for the best
in what matters.
Not third-rate.

Think, he said, what should be praised:
character, developed gifts,
a life lived inside-out
for love of God.
Not shameful.

～ Hang in There, He Said

Hang in there:
spin your web,
that intricate weaving
of who you are.
Wait there
in the interval
between up and down,
swaying in the wind,
hanging on by threads
that hold you in place.
Do what I made you
to do —
be what I made you
to be.
Rest there
in the caresses
of my breath
while I take care
of the world
spinning around you,
the hum of flying things,
the babble of masses.
Hang in your silent space
and wait,
ephemeral,
here today, gone tomorrow,
but my design.
Mine.

～ All I Have is Yours

This month you told me
to hold lightly to possessions;
that all I have is yours.

Then you brought me
chances to let go:
my sweater to the shivering boy,
my shirt to the cadaver
(swollen past the size of her own clothes),
my mat to the child who had no bed,
my socks to help the traveler.

Yes, all I have is yours.

❧ Praying Hosea 11

Father!

Against all expectation
(your sovereign majesty and
your station far above us),
you choose to be our *father*.

Abba!

You loved us when we toddled,
reached down to take our fingers
in your own tender handclasp
to walk us, gently crooning.

Our parent!

Your heart is soft, so tender
you put aside your anger
and offer us forgiveness—
calling, "Dear one, please come home!"

My daddy!

You bend to take my burden.
You lead with lovingkindness.
You feed me Bread from heaven—
delight me with your love.

⌇ Open Up or Hold Back?
(Isa 54:2)

Here on the threshold
of my tent
I pause, reluctant,
fear of
failing showing
in my trembling
fingers.
My hands grasp
the tent flaps
anyway
hoping I've heard right —
hoping he said
to open up,
throw back the curtains,
stretch the walls
wide open,
live with the inside
alive on the outside,

undone,
uncovered, inside out,
his remodeling there
for all to see.
If I hold back
cowering, covering
my flanks
as though I'm naked,
I'll miss out on
his plan.

Sunlight beats in beams
upon my fragile doors
knocking
to get in and flood
my indoor shadows —

tumbling
in on living wind
that breathes out
wholeness,
brings in loved ones,
his beloved,
who need love
within the camp, safe
inside my pavilion.

Don't hold back!
His words are clear.
I hear.
I lift the tent flaps,
tie them back
with ribbon
and step over
the threshold,
free at last to see

beyond me to
countless possibilities
of life
without fixed borders,
closed dreams,
shut shutters.

I'm vulnerable, yes, but
open wide
to what he wants —
dealing with all weather,
whether wet or dry,
his love
my dwelling place,
his Presence
my great shelter.

～ Prayer Wrestler
(Col 4:12)

My eyes are open,
taking in the signs
of life, death, and danger.
You urge me to watch,
and so I straighten up,
spine stiffened versus sleep,
eyes on the radar.

When I see subtle green
appear across the screen
I take it to mean growth.
And I, so thankful,
turn to you to celebrate
with deep delight
the re-creation going on.

But when the marks
of danger rear their heads
and stealthily diffuse
to hide themselves instead,
I sound the loud alarm,
my senses focused,
waiting for my cue.

And when at last
it comes, and I leap up
to act, suddenly I'm
wrestling, my opponent
slippery and elusive,

my holds tentative, untried,
my coach's voice a whisper.

The struggle is not
one I'd choose. Clenched,
pressured muscles strain;
my heartbeat shrieks;
my lungs cry out for air
against the fumes that feed
my fear. I cannot see!

I'd rather be assigned
a far-off perch away
from battle. This is
in-my-face, up-close,
so personal my very self
is pummeled to a pulp.
I need a hero, desperately.

Of course that's who
shows up: my own Dear One
to wrestle too, to find
the grip that will not slip,
to see beyond the sweat
that stings my eyes
(or is it tears? it's all the same).

I'm wrestling, yes,
but not alone. My coach
is wrestler too. And
when I feel the energy
come back to weakened knees,
exhausted hands, I know
he's fighting, in my skin.

∽ New Clothes
(Isa 61)

Getting dressed has never been
so sweet!
Music soars down from his heart
to mine,
wraps me round in hallelujahs and
amens.
I gather swathes of healing,
brilliant
in the sunrise, and tie them to
my waist,
lap them gaily over shoulders,
feel them swirling over feet
that lift
and leap and twirl in glad delight.
And why? Because I AM has
chosen me
to be his own, thrown away
my rags
(torn, disintegrating into threads
and grime)
and burned them in his fire.
He says I am beloved! His
tenderness
is pearls around my throat and
silver
on my wrist and diamonds sparkling
on my fingers as he opens wide
the gates
to usher me into his courts. Inside,

he shuts the door on mourning and
despair,
calls out his love, announcing to the
universe
that I am his, and he is mine,
forever.
His hands hold out my crown,
gorgeous
in the light of his eyes, gleaming
golden
as he settles it onto my head
and smiles.
Oh freedom! The load I dragged
behind me
all those years has been removed.
The grief that soaked my soul
is gone.
Clean, strong, full of gratitude,
I take
my place in the throngs of the
liberated,
the masses of the exultant
repatriated.
And praise to the King is the
theme of
every lilting psalm we sing as
we dance.

~ 4 ~
WHEN IT'S HARD

⁓ Download

He sat beside me on the bench
beneath our tree. "It's been too long,"
I said. "It's been so hard. And how
can I now listen when my hearing's clogged
by sorrows ricocheting through the alleys
of my mind? Words rush to tumble out,
and they are all lament!"

His arm went round my tense, stiff shoulders.
His voice reminded me to rest, to rip off
every heavy weight that drags me down,
and lay them there on him. On his lap. Right then!
And so I did, struggling to detach each grief.
They pulled back, resistant, iron magnetized
to my distress.

Still, one by one I tore them off
by telling him what each one meant to me:
losses made more poignant by the stretch
of ocean or ongoing silences, concerns,
dear ones fractured and unhealed,
the gripping agonies of people all around us
in this sick world.

"So, Lord, how long?" His singers
all have known this tune, have flung it
in his face for centuries. I sang it too,
but then he cupped my chin and turned
my eyes toward his. I saw his tears,
welling from his surging spring
of deep undying love.

His peace crept gently into
the frayed fibers of my soul, made whole
once more by this recurring download
of my griefs into his heart. He knows.
He cares. And he still holds
the perilous careening of the universe
in his pierced hands.

⌁ Psalm on Mean Street
(Ps 23:3)

LORD, you guide me to right pathways,
chosen for me, leading me home.
You said it.
I believe it.

But LORD, these are mean streets.
The other travelers form cliques,
gossip,
unnerve me.

And you mentioned "level" paths.
There are potholes here, jagged, deep!
They laugh
when I fall.

Tell them off, LORD — they are disgracing you!
You sent me here, and I wear your name:
"messenger,"
"Christ-ian."

The hardest part for me to bear
is that they wear your name too:
"colleague,"
"believer."

The residents of these mean streets
throw dirt into the holes, meaning well.
Temporary.
Useless.

Rain falls, and torrents scoop away
the cover-ups. The pits remain.
We move on
still at risk.

So now, LORD, where am I to go?
I am exhausted and afraid.
It's dark here
and lonely.

I thought I was a distance runner
with a long, graceful stride.
I'm crawling,
on my knees.

This paradox is too much for me.
I want clean streets, neatly paved,
the company
of friends.

> *Dear one, I have the map in my hands,*
> *but you can't see it in the dark.*
> *Trust me.*
> *I can see.*

> *This is the one way to get from here*
> *to there: a mean street full of holes*
> *but chosen*
> *with you in mind.*

My love hovers, a shelter from storms.
My love encircles, protecting from pot shots.
I breathe strength
into your body.

I move your knees (they're your best feature!)
to worship as they crawl, growing
stronger,
surer.

And just around the corner is relief.
Almost there — keep pushing on ahead!
You won't
believe your eyes.

So don't give up! I know it's hard.
But I have plans that you won't want to miss.
These mean streets
are history.

∼ Refuge
(Ps 62)

Outside:

a tempest rages,

turning laughing ocean deeps

to raging waves that lash the coast

with vengeance, sucking at my knees.

I turn tail and run for home,

sodden and storm-whipped,

stumbling at last into

my safe place.

Danger:

insinuations,

truth spun silly on its head,

unfairness turning oxygen to poison.

I can't breathe for aching. I gasp

for honesty and find it here,

at last, with you. Your words

are clear, not

murky.

Inside:

you hug me home.

I wring the filthy water from

my heart and flush it with strong antidote.

Your love, undiluted, unpolluted, disinfects

and cleanses all my wounds. Power

enfolds me, walls of energy form

one unending shield

on every side.

Safety:

I rest in you.

Nothing can blast me here

where you are King and guard me

from whatever sabotage is hiding in the dark.

Light shimmers from your fires.

You are the saving of me.

You are my one

safe place.

∼ Pressure
(Ps 55:22, 103:13; Mat 11:28-29)

When the pressure gets so heavy
that it feels just like
a dense cloud falling
turning solid
pushing me down

I must turn to you Lord
throw it all over
onto your shoulders
hands off now
leave it there

let you take the reins
and the driver's seat
your love setting the pace
your hands choosing the way
to move on ahead

you know how much I can take
the load you set on me
is bearable
that is your promise
you care for your own

and I am one of yours
I breathe in deeply
let it out
settle into the rhythm
of your love song

love for the nations
love for me

∼ I Am That Ewe
(Isa 40:10-31)

I am that sensitive ewe
that cries out what she sees
lurking by the precipice,
then cowers in the shade,
hiding out, because the rams
turn to push her aside
and other ewes grimace
with disdain and shock.

Did I not see that danger?
Am I really that near-sighted?
I struggle along, at the edge.
But there are others with me:
my special mate and certain friends.
We move on with the flock
but carefully go silent.
Some think our tears are dew drops.

But as I rise, next morning,
I hear the shepherd call my name.
He has not left us lonely.
His staff reminds me: he alone
can guide me and protect me.
No one but him truly knows
what lurks behind thorn bushes,
or which cliff edges crumble.
I breathe out. Breathe in. Calmed.

⁓ Turning the Other Cheek
(Mat 5:39; Luk 6:29; Rom 12:19-21; Prov 12:20)

I heard you say to turn the other cheek.
So, not striking them back, I did,
quietly hoping the slaps would end.
But I've been slapped twice more, instead.

The red on my cheeks does fade away.
The hurt that remains is deep inside;
my heart feels bruised, misunderstood.
Is this all I should do? Just hide?

Silence, for now, is my one resort.
How can I win over evil with good?
My hope is in you, my counselor.
How can I show love like I should?

It is yours to avenge. That you have said.
And you will repay. You gave your word.
My job is to wait, to promote peace.
So I will practice what I have heard.

∽ In the Wind
(Isa 44:8)

Wind whips wisps of hair
into eyes blurred by despair;
gusts grab my pulsing heart.
Nearly toppling,
scrambling for safe purchase,
I scream . . .

Then I hear:
Don't be afraid!
Stand up,
throw roots
to deep soil,
twirl them 'round
all obstacles —
further down,
further in,
drinking in
my love.
Know that
I AM
here
with you,
aware,
active inside
the twisters,
working
my rescue plan!

I rise, reach out,
send soul tendrils
into the silence
of rich loam,
plunge them further
into firm foundations,
waiting to see
what he's weaving
in the wind.

∽ The Cleansing
(Ps 37:7, 46:10; Exo 14:14)

I stand in the wind
while it whips along,
plastering my body
with fine dust,
the powdered aftermath
of life and death
and thirsty earth.
Deadwood and seedpods
hit the roof, my legs.
Birds of prey swoop overhead
looking for the innocent,
uncovered, to devour.

O Wind of God,
protect your own!
Hover over, cover us!
Breath of Life, strengthen us!
Heart of Sun, empower us:
your heat, our hope;
your air, our health;
your still small voice
our Word of choice,
while all around us
innuendo and
assumptions swirl!

I brush dust from my face.
His breeze flies by,
consoles my soul
then shivers all the trees
with swoops of power.
The Spirit breathes
and lifts away debris.
The land is swept,
cleaned up and clarified.
I watch. I wait. I listen for
the Whisperer,
my heart's desire.

> *Be quiet now;*
> *remember who I am,*
> *and that I rule.*
> *Wait patiently for me.*
> *Let go of your concern*
> *regarding those*
> *whose schemes succeed.*
> *My strength is*
> *all you need.*
> *I fight for you,*
> *and you, my child,*
> *need only to be still.*

∼ The Watched Pot
(Mal 3:3)

They're getting away with murder again,
words killing as surely as poison,
control choking off all life,
putting their spin on things while,
unnoticed,
the Body shrivels and dies.

So when will you act, LORD?
You are judge and sentencer,
and yet we see them winning
without just consequences.
I'm terrified.
Things are out of hand.

The refiner, meanwhile, unperturbed,
stokes the fire beneath the pot.
The golden molten metal shimmers.
A writhing blackness rises,
separates,
and the refiner scoops it out.

No lightning blast will serve the purpose.
This job requires caution,
meticulous heat adjustment,
a scrupulously watched pot
lovingly,
sternly stirred till it is pure.

∼ The Rain
(Hos 6:1-3)

Arrogant at heart,

self-sufficient,

my orientation is the desert.

Parched, cracked earth

turns to powder

and blows away,

transient, insubstantial.

Then, heart wide open,

vulnerable,

I turn to a pregnant sky,

and living water

drenches me,

quenches thirst

and soaks my soul solid.

Inside, I live
in fertile lands,
where forests flourish
in lavish rain.
He comes to me
as surely as
day breaks night sky to dawn.

~ 5 ~

HEARING THE VOICE
IN NATURE

∼ Look Up

Look down, and you see
withered leaves
parched gravel
litter blown in
caught on crushed twigs
death, thirst and brokenness.

Look up, and you see
the tent of love
I'm making you:
tiny green popcorn
exploding each hour
to dangle in grapes of gold.

Remember, hope is high
above your world
and only seen
when you decide
to focus upward
to what I'm weaving for you.

∼ Higher Things

Even tiny finches
live in a dimension
far above mine—
perching on light poles,
playing among tree blossoms,
drinking sweet nectar.
But you, Lord, also call me
to higher things,
to not stay prisoner
to dust and traffic
and corruption.

> You say my name
> and my soul rises
> to meet with you.
> You give me
> a panoramic view,
> instilling understanding
> in place of hopelessness.

You take my deep fatigue
and heal it with sweet rest,
the kind where
I lay back
onto your chest,
and when you lift me up
to soar like a small
clinging eaglet
I know your wings
hold me aloft.

You own the skies
as well as earth.
I watch the birds
slice the high reaches
and remember,
joy rising,
that – with you –
I can fly.

~ Reminder to My Soul

The town sounds are happy today:
    children cheering their soccer teams,
    hot percussion thumps from the *maquis*,
    women at the well, grateful for water.
This is a day that the Lord has made,
    I, too, will sing and be glad in it.
    His breeze pushes back the beating heat,
    his grace makes the blossoms pop for joy.
He brings one white butterfly to dance
    among the bobbing leaves,
    reminder to my soul to breathe,
    absorb the beauty and take heart.
He transforms sadness into melody
    and teaches me to fly inside his love.

∿ What I Would Rather Be

Sometimes my soul is all butterflies
flitting floating settling only
once in a while – briefly – to rest.

I would rather be the sentient head of seed
on the slender stem of grass
bowing gently to the breathing air.

∼ This Is What I Hear Today

This is what I hear today:

- dove song, *bulbuls*, greeting dawn

    and the Master of rotation,
    darkness yielding to the sun

- sons of Adam, daughters of Eve,

    stepping into community,
    finding the rhythm of tasks today

- thrumming hum of motors

    servant to their drivers
    or their riders, moving out

- rustling of a careful breeze

    shaking hands with mango leaves
    and the stalks of ripening corn

- the Voice that whispers wordlessly

    but hugs the contours of my soul
    to tell me yes, that I am his

∽ Morning Shade

Lord my God,
you are Spirit,
the wind brushing
the laughing leaves
and whooshing cool
safe shade over
my longing heart.

Yahweh, LORD,
you are the Breath,
the very air I breathe
filling my lungs,
oxygenating my soul
so that I live
in you, through you.

Jesus, Savior,
You come to me
invisible, but
real beyond
what I can touch,
you touch me
and I come alive.

I sit in morning shade
and find you here.

∾ Morning Hope

Thank you for green filaments waving in the breeze,
for silver sunlight filtered through overcast skies,
for the solid round edges of mangoes still ripening,
hanging pregnantly from bowed branches,
and for those that have turned to gold and fallen
to thirsty earth to make new wine and maybe children.

Thank you for the shower of petals on my path to work,
making a vibrant carpet for your scribe to tread,
each blossom individual in its watercolor variations
on themes of white and yellow, cream and rose and melon,
each one a witness to your great imagination
and artistic virtuosity, far beyond our imitations.

Thank you for soul music in the deeps of night
when thoughts carouse and wonder and weep;
you caress my distressed mind and stir in confidence
in your great story, the one that is not finished yet,
that holds my dear ones in your constant grip
and patiently designs a future filled with hope.

Thank you for reminding me this morning via mangoes
and frangipani season and the gift of nature's colors
and air movement in the pressured heat of April
that you are always here and there and everywhere.
You love us and delight in our anticipation of
the masterpieces you are creatively painting.

∼ Daybreak Shower

Quivering in delight
the green shafts shiver
and diamond droplets
roll tenderly down the leaves
swishing away the powder
of parched earth.

The heat has been
insidious, molten,
lying heavily on soul and soil
until we gasped for air.
Now we lie back
and let the cisterns fill:

drumroll on the tin roof,
melody of shifting wind
and birdsong in the shower,
background music to
the Voice that whispers
peace inside the hour.

∾ Cool Breeze

Cool breeze, breath of fresh air,
transforming muggy morning
into peace and delight –
so the Spirit blows, too,
Breath of God, moving,
changing the world, massaging hearts,
rustling words of wisdom and light
to anyone listening,
to anyone watching
the dust fly away
and leaves dance with joy.

∼ Stillness

(at Le Rucher in France)

You pressed silence
onto the frenzied fever
blistering my soul-skin,
a cooling compress
to cover cacophony.
Quiet slipped into pores,
over time, under tempest,
de-tensing every fiber.

At last, I heard the stillness,
not without sound, but
tendered by your touch
on the strings, keys,
surfaces of instruments
played softly by the lake:
chickadee and heron,
oak leaves shushing in the wind.
When clouds mounded
on mountains, and shards of sunset
shimmered pink on snow,
soft stripes in twilight,
I heard the Maker singing

warmth into these frozen ears.
The wrong cold melted,
firelight flamed its heat inside.

It was a time apart,
to turn me right-side out
and tame my wildness
into a listening love,
daughter sitting at your feet
with no agenda but
to be there in the solitude,
surrounded, not by furor,
but by you.

~ 6 ~
THE CONVERSATION

∾ When I Pray

when I pray
turning my heart
into position
for this day
you are here

we intersect
the Highest with
this needy one
beloved
adopted

this is the
holy crossroads
where two worlds meet
come together
walk as one

sacrifice[1]

not needed here

you paid the price

life itself

to own me

[1] In the Nyarafolo religious tradition in Côte d'Ivoire, a crossroads is a kind of spiritual portal, an optimal place to offer a sacrifice in a pot.

∿ Prayer Circle: Jesus Intercedes
(Rom 8:34)

He's not saying
he will beg the Father
on my behalf.
The Father loves me.

When he intercedes
he will be lifting me
into his lap for blessing,
or they might converse
about how much I've grown
and how to grow me next,
or he will be offering, as always,
his purity as covering for
my shame.

When I have needs
and come to him for answers
in his name,
he will corroborate my right to ask
because I'm his,
because I love him.
Their one heart will hold me close
within the circle of these prayers.

～ A Table Set Before Me
(Ps 23:5)

Dust swirls on the steppe, brushing barren paths
barer still,
twisting away like hope from my heart.

Danger lurks everywhere. I'm not alone,
but that is
why fear tempts me; these are not all friends.

Some carry knives. Some have it in for me.
Some don't care.
Others think I'm playing children's games.

And then you say, "Come eat!" and spread clean cloth
on the rock,
makeshift table in the wilderness.

It's set with china, fired by the hot sun's
noonday glares
and the enemy's flares. Unparalleled.

I sip ambrosia squeezed from suffering,
exquisite
flavors pressed from courage and despair.

The bread you slice is made from grains that died,
a thousand
crushed to powder, mixed with oil of joy.

Those faithful ones have given their hearts' blood
to make this
solid meal, a feast for Followers.

I eat my fill and find, like them, that you
alone can
satisfy. Your love removes all fear.

Some people see me, hand to mouth, and think
it's pretense,
wishful thinking making up this scene.

They only see the austere rock face, bare,
a woman
scooping empty handfuls of hot air.

They will not taste and see, and so with eyes
averted
they walk by, for fear it might be true.

∽ Mourning
(Ps 42:7; Mat 5:4)

May you, the God of peace
instill your peace in me,
these days of precious rest!

As Deep calls to deep,
I'll let go of struggling
and rest in you,

knowing that you
know more deeply
than I can guess

the ins and outs
and tormented depths
of my longings.

Heart and mind,
body and soul, I'm yours.
Grace me! Please!

"Blessed are those who mourn."

∽ Sensing God

We worship in a cloud, unfocused
though we strain to see and feel
yet worship what we know
within unknowing, all our senses
clamoring for the Real:

> — the One who touches hearts
> with joy, whose fingers reach to heal
> the blinded eyes, deaf ears;
> who feels our hurts because he hurt
> as human-Godson, heart and soul.

> — the One who sees me,
> eyes alert to know and care for me,
> penetrating always to the core,
> not fooled by the hypocrisy
> I put on like a suit, looking good.

> — the One who hears me,
> bending down to listen to my ramblings,
> sorting out the whimpers from the whines
> and hearing what the heart
> most surely needs for health.

— the One who smells
the fragrance of my praise, and blends it
with the songs of angels to concoct
aromas that unfurl in galaxies
and waken dances in the stars.

— the One who made
the amber sweet of honey, salt's allure,
hid cinnamon and coffee in the plants
along with things like pepper's hot surprise,
and calls to me to taste his treats.

He is the God of all the senses,
never numb to what concerns
his own. I pray. He comes,
he hears, he speaks, he enters me
and holds me in his never-ending love.

∼ Taste the Glory!
(Rom 8:23; Ps 90:14)

Taste the glory!

The very Breath of God
inhabits me,
holds my soul,
permeates my mind,
transforms my heart.

His touch is whisper-soft
behind the conscious
verbiage, constant
inner conversation.
My appetite is piqued.

I listen to the wind,
wait for sentience
to unlock the starving
fibers of my soul
to free delight in him.

Heat gradually turns up
to pulsing flame
and then I hear my name,
and hot and sweet joy
sizzles in my heart.

I feel the edge of heaven
at my feet. Someday
I'll float within
the ocean of his love,
possess as I'm possessed.

His radiance will be
my sun, burn fiery hot
but never harm,
just fill the world
with overwhelming glory.

I taste the flame
from far away
and find it pure
ambrosia, fit
for children of the God.

An endless feast
is waiting. Now
I nibble as I can,
his love the flavor
of forever —

and I am satisfied.

GLOSSARY

ant lions: these net-winged insects live in dry habitats. Adults have a very short life span, but their larvae are well-known for the cone-shaped pits they dig in order to trap passing ants or other insects. One step onto the sandy side of the cone and they slide to the bottom point, where they are caught and devoured.

balophone: a West African percussion instrument like a xylophone, with gourds tied under the wooden keys as resonance chambers. They are pentatonic and come in different sizes, some having as many as 21 keys.

bulbuls: a medium-sized songbird found across most of Africa and into Asia.

coucals: this designates multiple species of birds in the cuckoo family found across Africa, into southern Asia and also in Australia and the Solomon Islands.

hesed: this Hebrew word, in the Old Testament, refers to an essential attribute of God. Translations struggle to accurately express its deep meaning. Examples of English approximations are: loyal love, steadfast love, unending love, lovingkindness, mercy, faithfulness, loyalty.

maquis: in West African French, it refers to a small bar-restaurant.

Printed in the United States
by Baker & Taylor Publisher Services